Barnyard Buddies

In the Pig Pen

by Patricia M. Stockland
illustrated by Todd Ouren

Special thanks to content consultant:
Roger Stockland, Farmer/Rancher
B.S. Agricultural Engineering, South Dakota State University

visit us at
www.abdopublishing.com

Published by Magic Wagon, a division of the ABDO Publishing
Group, 8000 West 78th Street, Edina, Minnesota 55439.
Copyright © 2008 by Abdo Consulting Group, Inc. International
copyrights reserved in all countries. All rights reserved. No
part of this book may be reproduced in any form without
written permission from the publisher. Looking Glass Library™
is a trademark and logo of Magic Wagon.

Printed in the United States.

Text by Patricia M. Stockland
Illustrations by Todd Ouren
Edited by Jill Sherman
Interior layout and design by Todd Ouren
Cover design by Todd Ouren

Library of Congress Cataloging-in-Publication Data
Stockland, Patricia M.
In the pig pen / Patricia M. Stockland ; illustrated by
Todd Ouren ; content consultant, Roger Stockland.
        p.cm. – (Barnyard buddies)
Includes index.
ISBN 978-1-60270-025-3
1. Swine—Juvenile literature. I. Ouren, Todd.
II. Stockland, Roger. III. Title. IV. Series.
SF395.5.S75 2008
636.4—dc22
                                        2007004691

The barn is warm. A pen is covered in fresh straw.

Oink, oink, oink.

The sow grunts at her new piglets.

The sow and her piglets use the straw
as a bed. It keeps them warm and dry.

The litter has just been born. These piglets have pink skin covered in soft bristles.

A litter may have 12 or more piglets.

Piglets drink milk from their mother. The piglets nestle side by side to nurse.

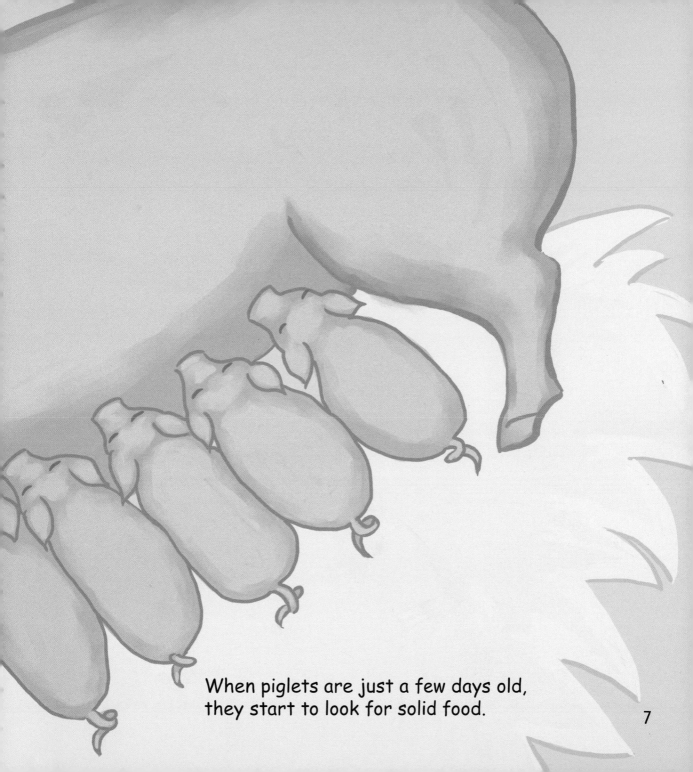

When piglets are just a few days old,
they start to look for solid food.

Soon, the piglets are big enough to leave their pen. They go outside and root in the mud.

8

Pigs root in mud to stay cool.
They also root for food.

9

The pigs spend their days rooting for food.
They also rest in the shade.

Pigs must stay cool. They have no
sweat glands to help them cool off.

11

As they get older, the piglets become adult pigs. Their bristles become hard. Their skin becomes tough.

Hard bristles and tough skin help protect pigs from sharp objects and biting insects.

13

At chore time, the farmer feeds the pigs. The pigs get grains and meal. This food helps the pigs grow big.

Pigs will eat almost anything. Farmers
usually feed pigs corn, meal, and
other grains.

When it is time for the pigs to sleep, they return to their pens. The pigs root under the dry straw. The straw makes a nice blanket for a pig.

Pigs will sleep together if
the weather is chilly.

17

When the pigs are all grown up, they will be separated. Some will go to market. Some will stay at the farm and have more piglets.

Farmers raise pigs for
their meat and hides.

For now, the pigs enjoy their days of mud and shade.

Oink, oink, oink.

Pig Diagram

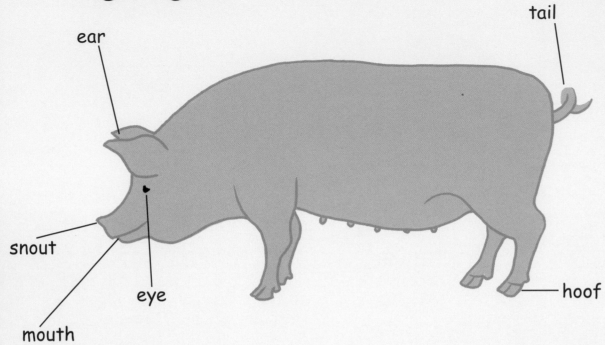

ear

tail

snout

eye

mouth

hoof

Glossary

bristle—hair.
market—where animals are bought and sold.
nurse—to drink milk from a mother animal.
root—to turn up the ground in search of something.
sow—an adult female pig.
sweat gland—part of the skin that makes sweat to
                          help keep an animal cool.

Fun Facts

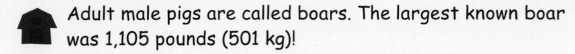 Adult male pigs are called boars. The largest known boar was 1,105 pounds (501 kg)!

Not all pigs are pink. Some breeds are red. Others have spots. Some even have a stripe around their belly.

Pigs are very intelligent, curious animals.

Pigs are very clean animals. They will always use the same corner of their pen for the bathroom. Pigs will not lie down in manure if they can help it.

Pigs can grow tusks, which are like teeth. These tusks can be very sharp.

Wild pigs are related to domestic pigs.

Pigs have an excellent sense of smell. Their snouts are also very strong. Pigs help people find truffles buried in the ground.

In addition to oinking, pigs grunt and squeal.

Index

bristles 4, 12, 13
farmer 14, 15, 19
food 6, 7, 9, 10, 14, 15
litter 4, 5
market 18
mud 8, 9, 20
pen 3, 8, 16

piglet 3, 4, 5, 6, 7, 8, 12, 18
root 8, 9, 10, 16
shade 10, 20
skin 4, 12, 13
sow 3, 6
staying cool 9, 11
straw 3, 16